INTRODUCTION TO
FASHION DESIGN

PATRICK JOHN IRELAND

B.T. Batsford Ltd · London

ACKNOWLEDGEMENTS

The author would like to thank everyone who helped in compiling this book, in particular, the staff and students of Bournemouth College of Art and Design; The Principal: A. J. Marshall, for his generous help in giving permission to photograph the School of Fashion; Head of School, School of Fashion: Clive Kirby, for his encouragement, advice and enthusiasm; Head of School, School of Photography: Sylvia Barnes for her helpful cooperation; In-house photographer: James Philip Howe, for his photographs of the Fashion Department and of students' work; Rainer Usselmann for the photographs on pages 4 and 5, and the students on the B. Tec National Diploma and Higher National Diploma courses for allowing me to show examples of their work.

I would also like to extend my thanks to Ann Ward for her helpful advice, Cordwainer's College for the photographs on page 37, my editors at Batsford, Richard Reynolds, Kate Bell and Thelma Nye, and finally to Sue Lacey, who designed the book.

SHREWSBURY
SIXTH FORM COLLEGE

NOV 1995

BOOK NUMBER B/4174

CLASSIFICATION 746.92

*Dedicated to
Alexander Reissner*

First published 1992
Reprinted 1993, 1995

© Patrick John Ireland, 1992

All rights reserved. No part of this publication may be reproduced, in any form or by any means, without permission from the publisher

Typeset by Servis Filmsetting Ltd, Manchester and printed in Hong Kong

Published by
B.T. Batsford Ltd
4 Fitzhardinge Street
London W1H 0AH

A CIP catalogue record for this book is available from the British Library

ISBN 0713460172

Patrick John Ireland
Photograph by Rainer Usselmann

The following pages give an introduction to the fashion industry which includes fashion drawing and presentation techniques.

First year
fashion show
at Bournemouth
College of
Art and Design

Students of fashion are introduced to a broad spectrum of the industry, combining creativity with the opportunity to study fashion design, pattern cutting and garment production. At the same time, they are given an insight into the world of fashion marketing and promotion. Project work includes visual study exercises and research into the design and manufacture of, for example, garments for casual wear, daywear, evening and sportswear. Visits to fashion exhibitions and trade fairs are encouraged, and visits to manufacturers' international fashion shows are arranged by the colleges.

Students need fashion drawing and presentation skills when developing design ideas in response to a brief and are taught different ways of presenting ideas when sketching, and how to produce working drawings suitable for pattern development and illustration. The general presentation of all work is strongly emphasized in the courses at all levels. The different methods of drawing and presenting work are illustrated, as relevant, throughout this book.

5

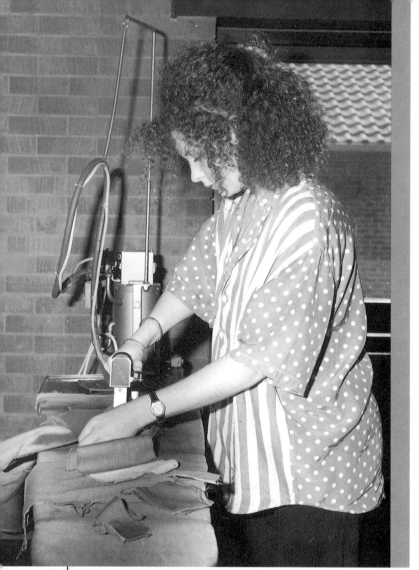

TRAINING AS A FASHION DESIGNER

Any student wishing to become a fashion designer should first apply to take a fashion design course at a college or polytechnic. Many education establishments all over the country offer courses which vary in length from one to four years, depending on the qualifications required. As well as training students in the creative and technical aspects of the subject, some courses include a period of work experience in the fashion industry to give students the opportunity of working in the commercial world. Courses also include visits to factories of fashion houses, and exhibitions in both Great Britain and overseas. Detailed information is given in the relevant college prospectuses and students wishing to apply for a course should write for and complete an application form. If short-listed, an interview will be arranged at which a portfolio of work should be shown.

PORTFOLIOS FOR INTERVIEWS

Preparing a portfolio for an interview requires careful planning to make it easy for the interviewer to look through the work. Arrange the material with care, selecting only your best work. Make sure that you are able to explain any details clearly should you be asked to do so. Colleges will often give a guideline as to what they are looking for in relation to the work they wish to see.

It is important to date all work according to when it was produced.

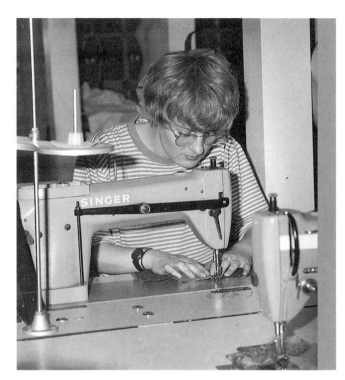

DESIGN COMPETITIONS

While studying on a fashion course, the colleges enter students of fashion design for competitions sponsored by clothing or textile companies.

Students have the opportunity to design for many different areas of fashion from sportswear, day and evening wear to more specialized areas. This gives them the experience and challenge of entering a competition and the possibility of winning a prize. Incentives are offered to those who are successful in competitions, and these may take the form of financial reward, and sometimes the opportunity of employment after leaving college.

The pictures in this section were taken in the studios of students on the B.Tec. Diploma course at Bournemouth College of Art and Design.

DESIGNING A COLLECTION

There are two main fashion seasons a year: Spring/Summer and Autumn/Winter. Each season requires a different image and a range of styles and colours.

The designers need to work about twelve months in advance so, in the Spring they will be working on the Spring/Summer collection for the following year and in the Autumn for the following year's Autumn/Winter collection. As soon as one collection is complete, they begin work on the next collection.

DESIGN PROJECTS

Students of fashion design are given design projects set by their college lecturer, by a manufacturer, professional designer or a buyer.

Each project will give students the opportunity to design in different areas of fashion. The design briefs are presented in a concise way explaining the requirements and stages in which to work, and when the project needs to be completed. It is important that students

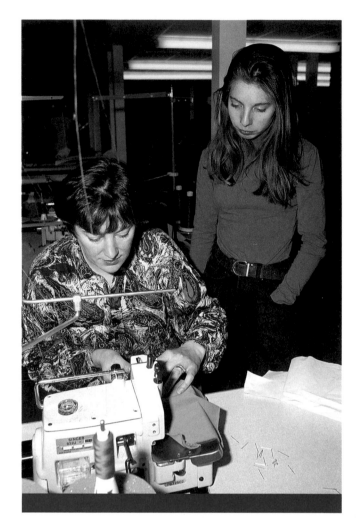

understand the brief fully before commencing, and interpret the requirements correctly. For example:

○ What exactly have you been asked to design?
○ For whom are you designing — a company, the consumer or a retail outlet?
○ On what occasion and in what environment would the garment be worn?

Points which will affect your design decisions:

○ How the work is to be produced.
○ Specific considerations stated in the brief.
○ The date when the work needs to be completed.

After marking, constructive criticism is given of the work submitted.

DESIGN RESEARCH AND SOURCES OF IDEAS

When developing research and looking for a theme on which to base ideas, the designer will look in many different areas. The following are a few suggestions for sources of ideas:

- films
- theatre
- television
- sports
- paintings
- nature
- history of costume – different periods of fashion
- national costume
- military uniforms
- street fashion (ideas that have not been taken up on a commercial level)

It is important that a designer is constantly aware of the changes and influences taking place in the fashion industry. Successful marketing and promotion is vital. They should also be aware of the effectiveness of fashion exhibitions, trade fairs and fashion shows. Advertising is also important and window display certainly plays a part. Fashion magazines should be thought of in terms of their readership and editorial content.

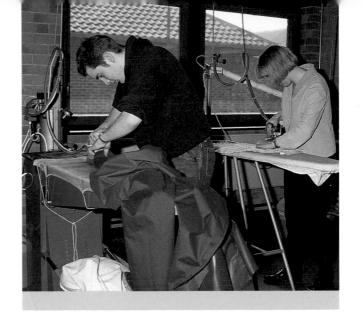

Students taking a fashion design course, work closely with specialists on their design projects and will usually be entered for nationally and internally sponsored competitions. Some colleges include specialized courses in different areas of the fashion industry, i.e. knitwear, textiles, embroidery, millinery, shoes and accessories, sportswear, marketing promotion, and management courses.

DIFFERENT AREAS OF WORK

When leaving college it is advisable to gain work experience with a company before considering freelance work.

Designers may work in one of three different areas:

Working in industry

In-house designers are fully employed by a fashion company.

Working freelance

Working as a freelance designer enables work to be sold to fashion houses, and direct to shops or to clothing manufacturers. The garments would have the buyer's label.

Setting up a company

Fashion designers may set up their own company. Many people find this more satisfying than working for someone else, as their designs are sold under their own label.

DIFFERENT AREAS OF FASHION

Haute couture

A couture garment is made specially for an individual customer. The fit and look takes priority over the cost of materials and time it takes to make.

Mass market

Ready-to-wear clothes in large quantities and standard sizes are made in inexpensive materials. The designs are imaginative and well represented in the High Street shops and stores.

Designer labels

These garments are not tailored to the individual customer but are produced in small quantities to guarantee exclusivity and tend to be expensive. They are labelled with the designer's name and reflect a distinctive style, with care taken in the cut and making up.

STARTING WITH THE BASIC FIGURE

Students require the ability to produce design ideas with clarity and speed. It is necessary to be able to sketch the figure with a few simple lines. It helps to calculate the height of the figure by estimating the number of heads into the body.

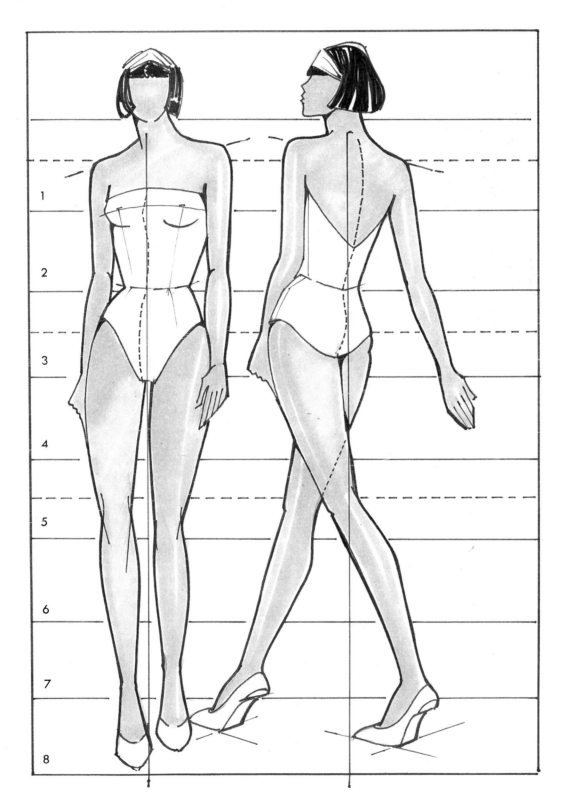

DRAWING WOMEN

In the average woman the head will divide into the height by about $7\frac{1}{2}$ times. For fashion sketches, the number is increased to 8 or $8\frac{1}{2}$ times. The length of the legs is often exaggerated but the figure itself should not be, as the design must relate to the whole figure. When design sketching it is not necessary to draw the face and hands in detail. Techniques vary from stylized drawings to a more realistic approach depending on the image required to project.

The vertical or balance line is drawn from the pit of the neck to the foot taking the weight of the body, to indicate that the head and neck are above the supporting foot. It is useful to draw this line very lightly when starting the sketch to obtain the correct balance.

Skill can be much improved by practising drawing from a model or by attending life classes and studying anatomy.

The figures illustrated give an outline of the female figure proportions. Consider the pose in relation to the image it is wished to project, i.e. sporty, sophisticated, active or casual.

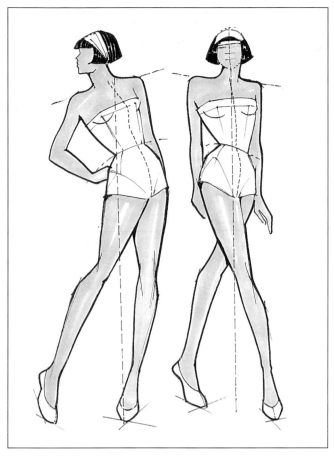

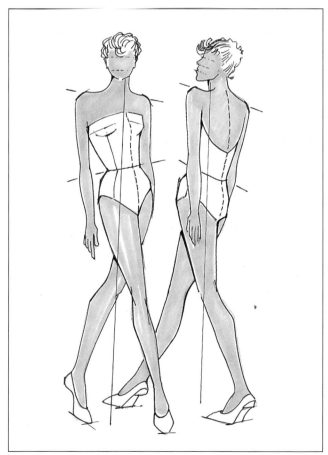

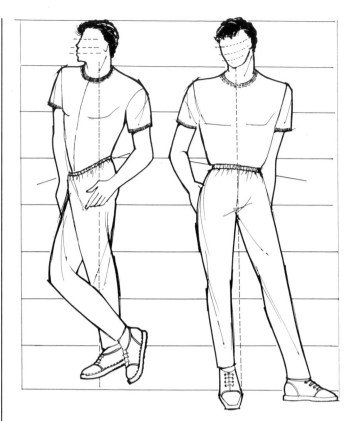

DRAWING MEN

The proportions for the male figure are $7\frac{1}{2}$ to 8 heads divided into the figure length. For fashion drawing purposes, as for women, the length of the legs is often exaggerated. Note the balance line used from the pit of the neck to the foot taking the weight of the body and the centre front line following the contour of the body.

Develop poses which enable the design to be made without spending too much time working on the figure. Note that front, side and back views are included.

Sketch from life or from photographs and magazine illustrations to develop new poses. Keep a file of photographs and cuttings for reference.

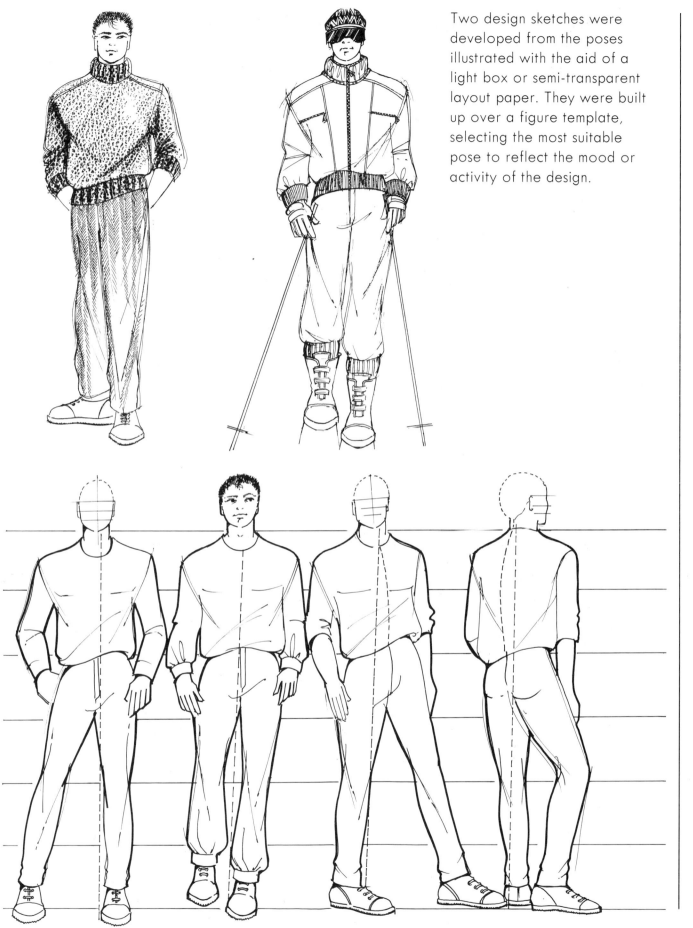

Two design sketches were developed from the poses illustrated with the aid of a light box or semi-transparent layout paper. They were built up over a figure template, selecting the most suitable pose to reflect the mood or activity of the design.

DRAWING CHILDREN

Many design sketches of children seen in publications are highly stylized, because it is difficult to draw children in a set pose as they are not very patient models. It is therefore better to make quick sketches from life or use a camera to capture some active poses, and then develop them later.

Experiment with different techniques of illustrating children from very stylized cartoon illustrations to a more realistic approach.

A selection of figure poses; note the balance line from the pit of the neck to the foot taking the weight of the figure.

These sketches were developed over figure templates using semi-transparent layout paper.

Note the construction lines sketched in lightly with a pencil and the final stage of the completed sketch, which uses a Pantone marker pen for the flesh tint and coloured pencils with a Pentel Ultra Fine line pen for the details.

Three sketches produced using the same pose to illustrate different designs.

17

When drawing children and designing for different age groups, it is important to be constantly aware of the changing proportions of the growing child.

The method illustrated (*right* and *far right*) will help the student to sketch the figure and work out the correct proportions to the age.

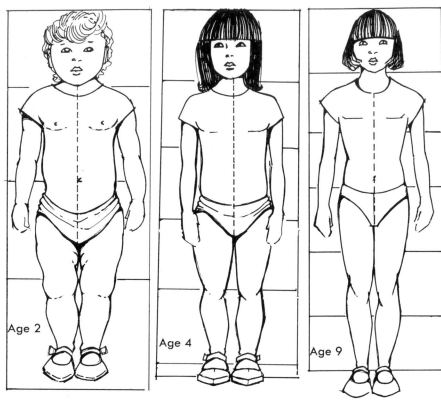

Age 2

Age 4

Age 9

This illustration has been developed in two stages using a Fine Pilot Hi-Tecpoint pen. First the outline of the figure is sketched in with a few lines using the balance line from the pit of the neck to the foot taking the weight of the pose. Then the details are added and sketched in with care. A pale grey marker pen is applied with a free technique to suggest folds and shadows, giving the sketch more depth.

Age 12   Age 15   Age 18

POCKETS

Pockets may be made up first and then stitched onto the outside of the garment or they may be made as part of the garment and concealed within it. The pocket may be used as a decorative feature on a design often with added details, such as pleats, gathers and seams.

Flap pockets are produced as a slit in the fabric. They may vary in size and position, may be cut horizontal, vertical or curved.

There are three ways of finishing a slit pocket. *Bound* which looks like a bound button hole; *Flap* which is inserted into the upper edge of the slash and *Welt* which is a separate piece of fabric sewn into the lower edge of the slit.

Patch pockets

21

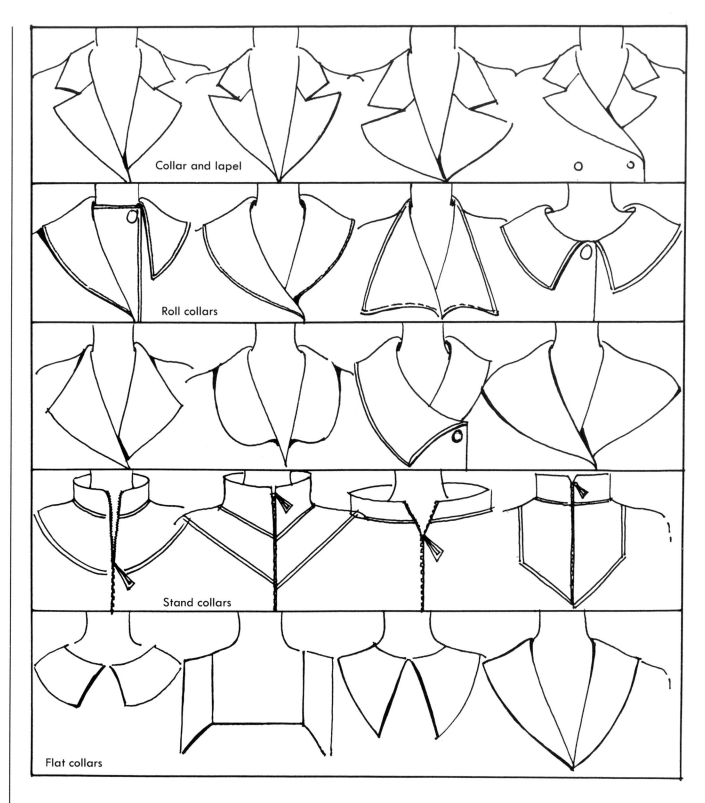

Collar and lapel

Roll collars

Stand collars

Flat collars

DESIGNING COLLARS

Collar designs are based on the basic styles —
flat, roll and stand — which may be attached to
the neckline, detached or convertible. The
weight and texture of the material used
produces different effects so this should be
considered carefully in design sketches.
This section illustrates a selection of designs
adapted from the three basic styles and from
which many variations may be developed.

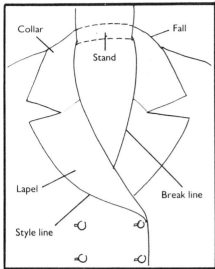

Collar / Fall

Stand

Lapel / Break line

Style line

This diagrammatic sketch indicates the terms used for different parts of the collar.

Develop designs in the sketchbook for future reference. Sketch collars seen at fashion shows, in shop windows and magazines, and keep a folder of different styles. Also refer to past periods of fashion for ideas, working from paintings, book illustrations and old films. A selection of styles is shown here.

DRAPES, FOLDS AND GATHERS

When representing folds, gathers and drapes it is important to understand the character of the fabric to be illustrated. The way in which it falls into folds depends on its weight and thickness. To have a real understanding of the material it is helpful to drape a selection of fabrics on a dress stand and study the way in which folds and gathers behave. Make sketches in line and colour using different media to achieve the effects required.

Note the way in which lightweight fabrics fall into small soft folds in contrast to those of the heavy and rich materials.

Frills, flounces, bias cut drapes

Note the way the skirt designs have been sketched, using a guideline for the hem of the skirt. A few lines will convey the type of material, drape, gathers or frills.

The sketches have been coloured with Stabilo softcolour pencils. Note the darker tones which give depth to the folds and drapes.

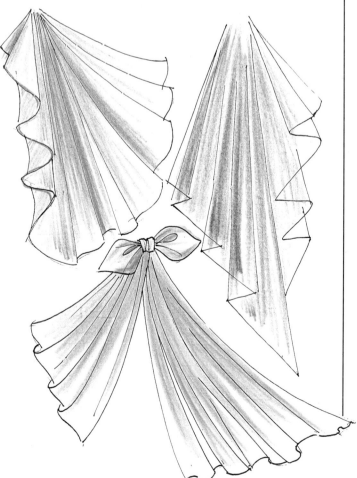

25

DESIGN SKETCHING USING A TEMPLATE

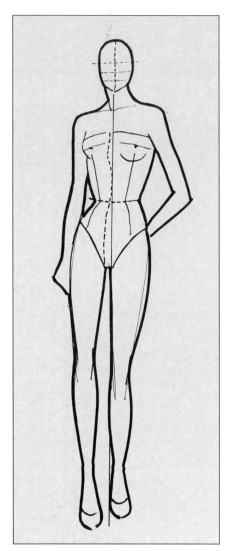

1. When using a figure template select a pose which is suitable for the design, e.g. elegant, sporty, casual or sophisticated, and draw on a semi-transparent layout paper or work over a light box so that the image of the template is seen through the paper.

2. Develop the design lightly over the figure with a pencil, bearing in mind the shape of the design in relation to the figure. Carefully place details, i.e. pockets, seams, fastenings, etc., using the centre front as a guideline to obtain the correct balance.

3. Complete the design by adding the final details. Consider the front and back views in relation to one another.

26

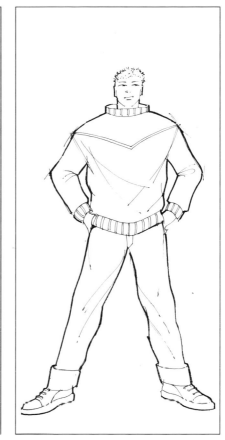

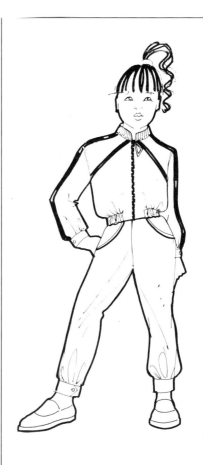

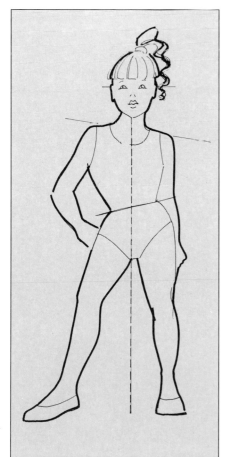

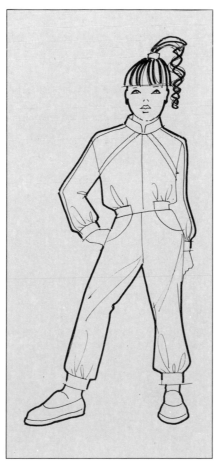

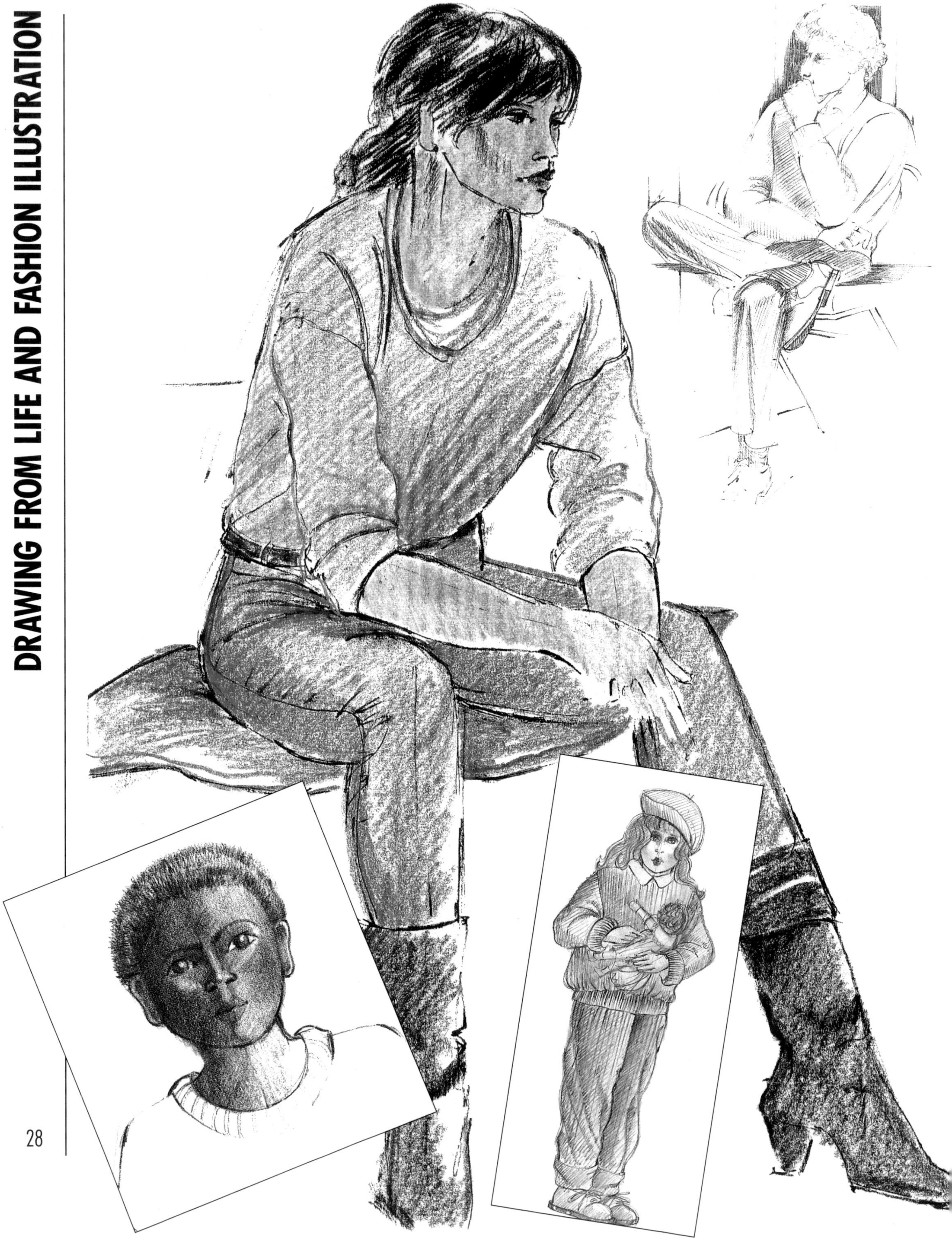

Most fashion design courses have a period allotted to life and fashion drawing.

The length of poses in the classroom will vary from five to twenty minutes but often a friend will be prepared to model for you. It is an advantage to create new poses working from the model and to study the behaviour of a garment when subjected to changing movement. Experiment using different media and types of paper, and try drawing in varying sizes, working from very free to more controlled techniques.

It is important for the fashion illustrator to be able to draw the whole figure and observe the general effects of the pose and main style details of the design.

It is good practice to sketch very short poses of two to five minutes, as often when attending fashion shows, designs need to be drawn quickly from memory. Notes of the designs should also be scribbled down, such as the fabric used, any special design features, and colour used.

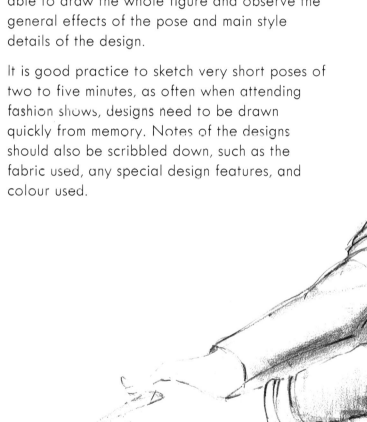

Many hat designs are based on a few basic styles with many variations, using different materials and trimmings, as shown in these sketches.

The hat is an important accessory to the total fashion image. The designer should start working on a theme producing a number of sketches developing ideas and suggesting materials and trimmings. From the sketches the hats are developed in the workroom, using different methods. The foundation fabrics and materials are draped and modelled on a wooden millinery block which is made in all relevant sizes.

A selection of some of the basic styles from which many variations are designed is shown here.

Picture hat

Boater

Breton

Flying

Trilby

Pillbox

Stetson

Cap

Scullcap

Note the way the hat has been drawn in relation to the head. It is helpful to construct a drawing with a few guidelines sketched in lightly with a pencil. These sketches have been produced with a soft Black Prince pencil.

The hats illustrated here have been produced with Pantone marker pens combined with Derwent coloured pencils. Note the construction lines indicating the position of the hat in relation to the head.

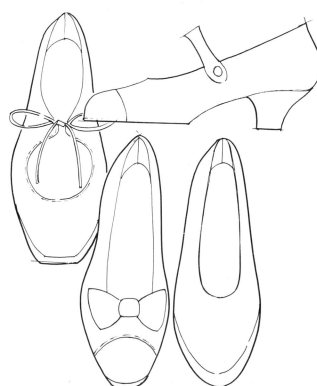

It is important to suggest the correct proportions of the foot in relation to the shape of the shoe design. Design sheets show the shoe from different angles and suggest the effects of textures and decoration in leather.

A selection of design sheets and presentation of shoe designs are illustrated in this section. It is good practice to select a number of shoes of different styles and make sketches of them, working from different angles. Note the variations of styles, shape of heels, and design details in your drawings.

Sketches produced in two stages:

1. Black line sketches illustrated using a Fineliner fibre-tipped pen.
2. Shading has been applied using a soft black Prince Pencil. Note the variation of tone and areas of white left to give the effect of light.

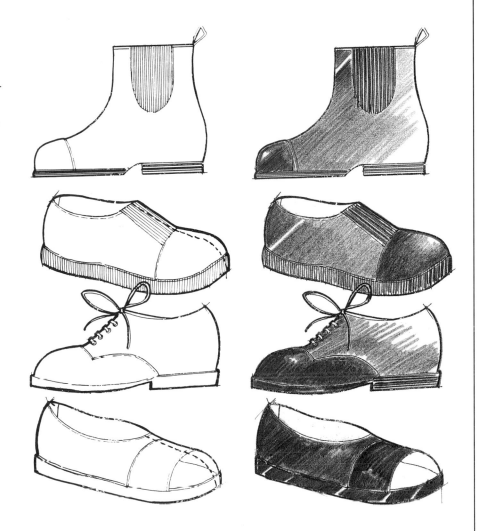

SHOE DESIGN DEVELOPMENT SHEETS

Drawing and designing shoes requires an understanding of the method by which they are made and the materials used.

The way in which the design sheets are produced depends on the individual. Full information is shown on the sheets illustrating the designs from different angles, together with samples of the materials to be used and explanatory notes added when necessary.

RESEARCH

When visiting museums, art galleries or exhibitions, buy postcards, and sketch anything which may be a suitable subject for research and design development.

Students taking a shoe design course are given a brief which would suggest the market, a type of shoe and the occasion for it to be worn. The research theme for ideas may be stated or left for the students to select.

The fashion image needs to be considered. First a complete understanding of the requirements of the design brief is essential. Then there is a period of research. Ideas often involve visiting museums, taking photographs, referring to books on such subjects as architecture, the history of fashion, decoration, and plant forms. Often a visit to an appropriate factory is arranged.

Students should always start by using a sketchbook. Often a research board can be made, from which to work when

Black leather boot. Black line drawings using two line values. Colour has been applied using soft wax pencils. Note the small areas of white left to suggest the shiny surface of the leather

Children's casual shoes. A selection of shoe designs produced in two stages

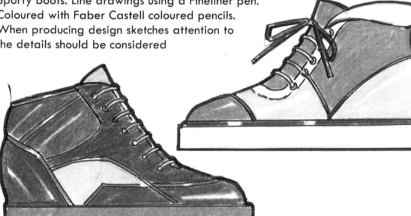

Sporty boots. Line drawings using a Fineliner pen. Coloured with Faber Castell coloured pencils. When producing design sketches attention to the details should be considered

developing design ideas, and samples should be made experimenting with different techniques.

From the research, sample design sheets are produced, working to the selected theme and developing many design sketches.

When one or more designs have been selected, a presentation drawing is often produced, illustrating the design in full colour with samples of leather and trimmings, and a fashion sketch suggesting the total image is often included.

The next stage is to produce a working drawing to be taken to the workroom for the shoe to be made up.

Students developing shoe designs in the workshop of Cordwainer's College

37

When starting a design collection students begin with design research, working from different areas searching for a theme. Inspiration may come from many sources, in fact from any object which has a strong visual impact. Students start by entering ideas in a sketchbook.

A camera may also be used to record images and textures of, for example, cloud formations, flowers and plant forms and architectural details.

Research material is often displayed on a pin board for quick reference when designing.

Sketchbooks are available in hardcover or softcover, with spiral binding, or tear off perforated sheets. The quality and type of paper varies from lightly textured to that with a smooth surface, but a good quality paper should take any medium adequately. The

Joyce Elias

sketchbook is a good starting point when beginning a design project. Sketchbooks are very important to fashion design students and should be a constant reference during their course and in continuous use throughout their careers. The sketchbook reflects students' work from areas of research for design ideas and inspirational themes, to colour

research, fabric samples, cuttings, notes and sketches.

In many colleges students start a project working in the sketchbooks, developing research and design themes and colour stories before taking the work to a more finished stage. Their sketchbooks are usually displayed, together with

completed project work, when making presentations for assessment.

The students whose work is shown here, are all from the first year B.Tec. Diploma course at Bournemouth College of Art and Design.

Sophie Wright

Juliet Bugler

When answering a design brief, students may be required to produce a storyboard reflecting the research, colour and fabric of a design collection.

FASHION PREDICTION BOARDS

These boards consist of photographs, fashion sketches, fabric samples and notes on design influences.

These boards are used professionally for promotional purposes when giving a presentation to clients and for display purposes on exhibition stands. They are also helpful for staff training, and to inform of new trends, colours and fabrics for the coming seasons. They are often photographed for fashion and textile magazines with articles promoting and predicting fashion trends.

COLOUR BOARDS

Colour boards are used to promote new colour combinations, together with fabric samples displaying patterns and textures.

PROFILE BOARD

This board is a customer profile reflecting the market research life style and environment in which the designs would be worn. Material is carefully selected to illustrate these points and photographs are often included to indicate the type of person for which the collection has been designed, e.g. sporty, sophisticated, elegant.

RESEARCH BOARDS

Students of fashion design will often be asked to produce a research board. The way in which material is arranged on the board, and the colour schemes selected, reflect the mood and theme being promoted.

The board should include carefully selected reference material consisting of, for example, photographs, photocopied material, postcards, magazine cuttings, sketches, and fabric trimmings, which serve as a source of reference and inspiration when designing.

FASHION DESIGN PRESENTATION BOARD

The board presents a collection of designs with fabric samples and working drawings and may also include sketches, photographs or any other relevant material to suggest the mood of the designs and the environment in which they would be worn.

A final presentation board comprising an illustration with working drawings and a background photograph is shown opposite.

A selection of storyboards produced by students of fashion is shown on the following two pages. (First Year B.Tec. Diploma course at Bournemouth College of Art and Design in the School of Fashion.)

SPRING/SUMMER 1991

ATLANTIS

44

Sally Ann Brown

Tiffany Curtis

SPRING/SUMMER 1991

CHILDRENS RESORT WEAR

Sara Petty

45

Design sheets are based on a theme and the sketches are developed by experimenting with the various designs.

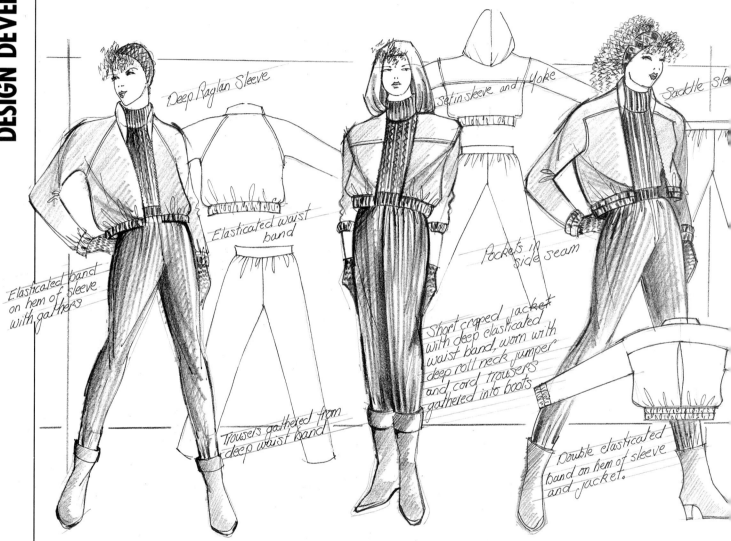

The style of drawings and layout of the sheets is up to the individual. As illustrated, some students and designers sketch freely whereas others tend to use a more stylized method. Both students and professional designers often save time by tracing over a figure template. This enables them to sketch with greater speed, but is a matter of individual choice.

Back views are included as well, and these could be diagrammatic or sketched on a figure. Colour and pattern are suggested, combined with notes giving additional information if the sketch is not self explanatory.

WORKING DRAWINGS

The importance of working drawings for production means that every detail of the design must be clearly shown. The sketch is usually a flat (front view) drawing which must be in proportion to the figure. The placing of details such as darts, seams, pockets and buttons need to be considered with care.

Silk jacket with hood
Deep round yoke.
Dropped shoulder line, gathered
waist band with drawstring tie
C.F. button fastening
3/4 length sleeves

Wool jersey jacket
Draped hood. Gathered waist
Full gathers. Patch Pockets.
Set in sleeves.

The working sketch is an analysis of the fashion sketch and the practical aspects of the design must be considered. For example, how the collar is attached, the type of fastening to be used, and the seam placement. When a design has an intricate detail this should be drawn separately with notes explaining any points which it may not be possible to express clearly in the drawing.

47

AFRICA

A festival of colors

Steven Cocker BA (Hons)

This research board, on the theme of Africa, was the inspiration for a sportswear collection using African motifs and colours.

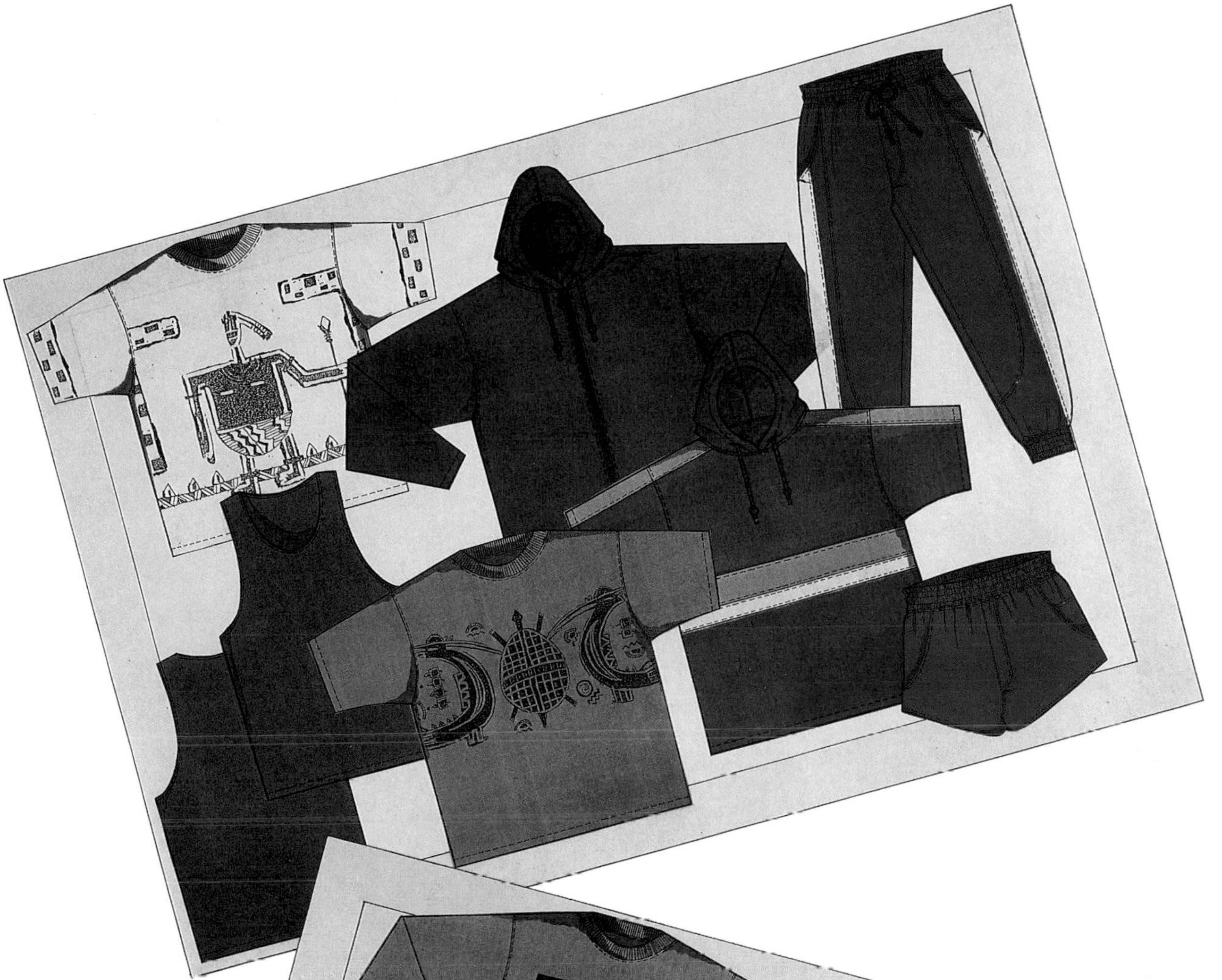

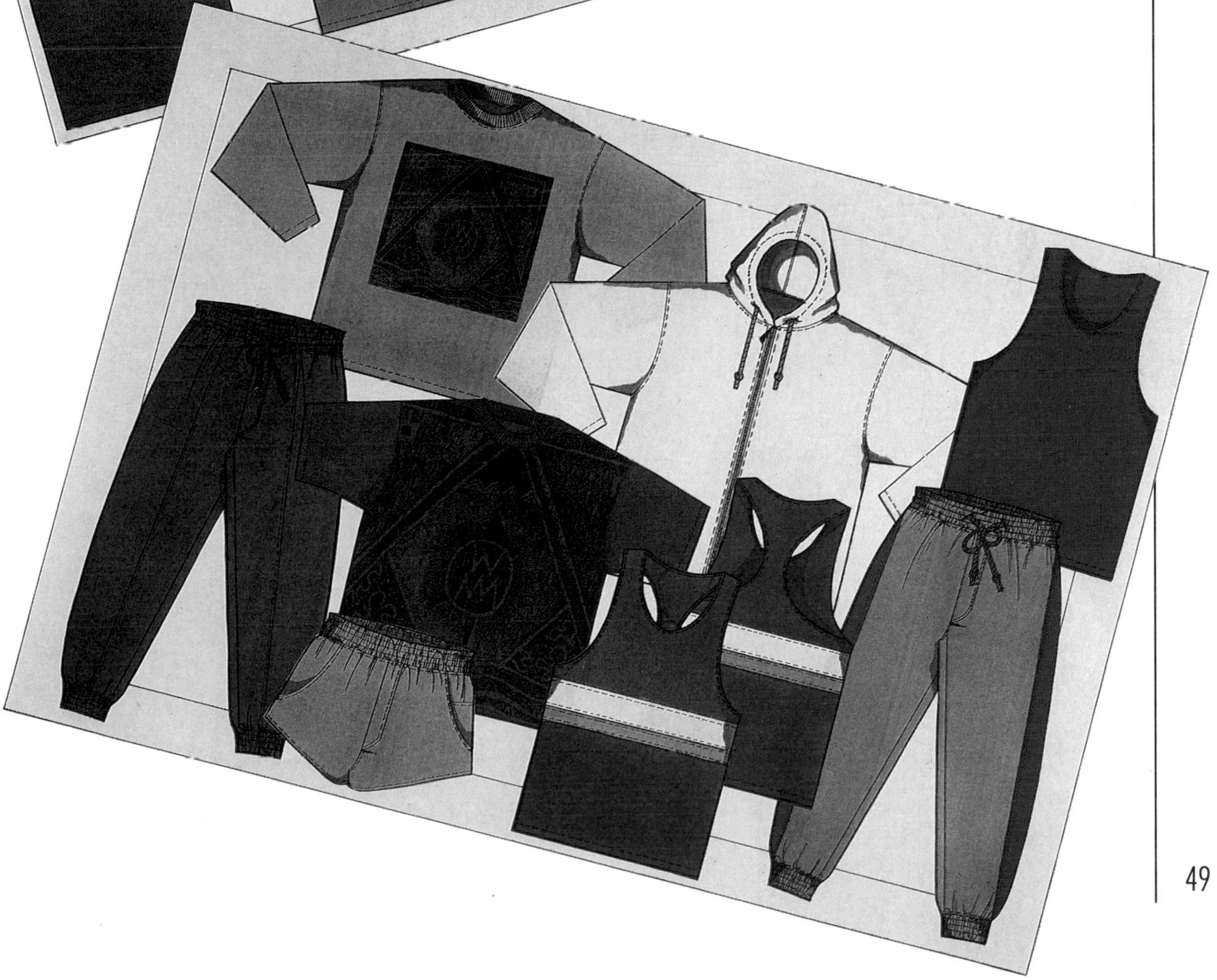

When developing different textures, it is not necessary to produce a pattern in great detail; a suggestion is all that is required on a design sketch. When working on a presentation drawing or illustration it may be necessary to illustrate the pattern in more detail, reducing it to the scale of the sketch.

It is a good experience for students to make a fashion sketch and reproduce it a number of times (a photocopier may be used), and experiment on each sketch working from a selection of sample patterned fabrics.

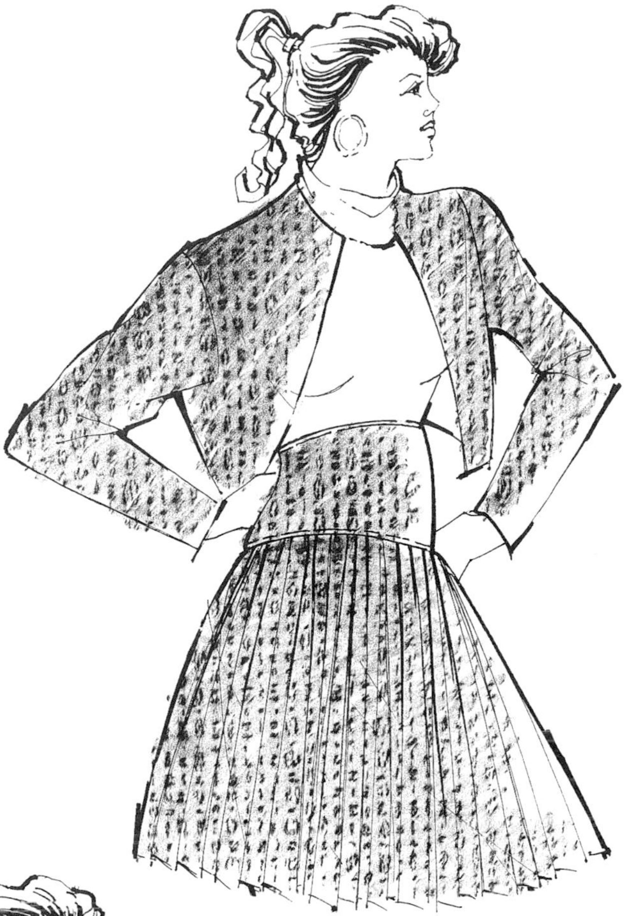

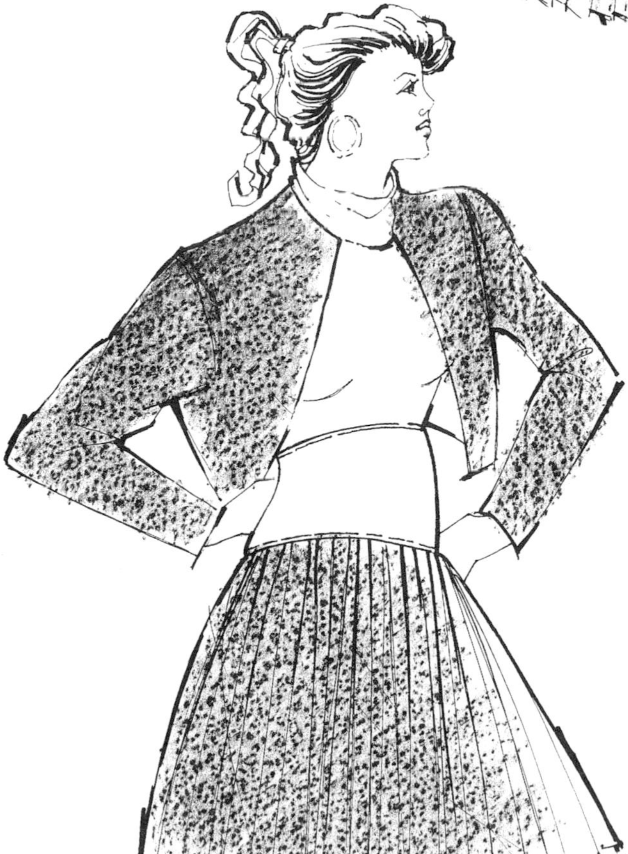

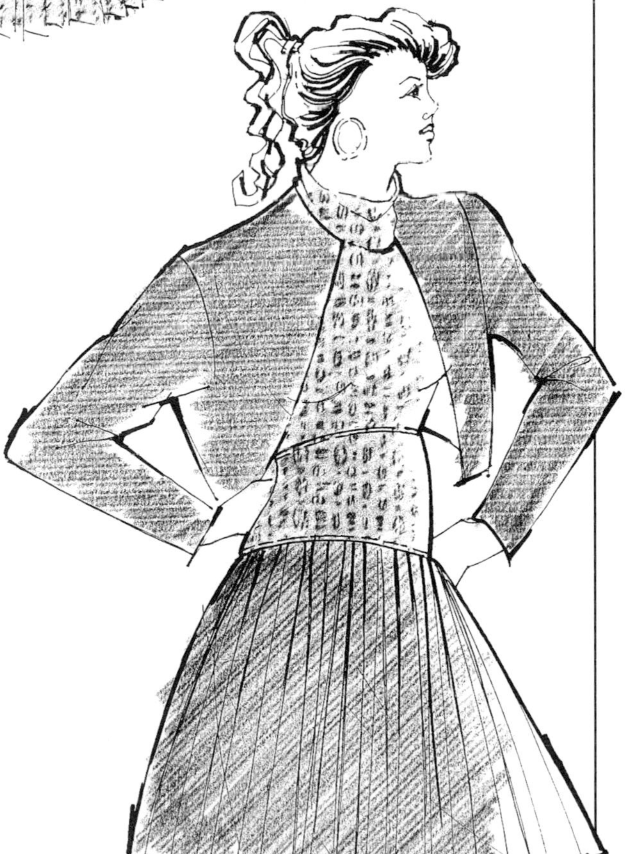

Experiment with different media to achieve a variety of effects.

Match the colours against the fabric being used. It is most effective to work on one side of the figure in darker tones, with lighter tones on the other side, to give more contrast and shape.

52

There is a large selection of art materials from which to choose when designing and illustrating. Some of the more popular materials are listed in this section with examples of work shown. It is important to experiment with different materials, trying out different effects and exploring new possibilities.

The cost and quality of art materials vary. It is therefore advisable for students to select very carefully the materials they require. It is not always necessary to buy large quantities, and such items as marker pens, pencils, inks, and pastels may be purchased individually or in small packs.

It is important to take care of the materials and to make sure before working that the pencils are sharp, the pens clean, and the brushes and mixing palettes washed and dry, ready for use. Marker pen caps should always be replaced as the marker tends to dry out quickly.

Keep all materials in a box and in good order so that they are readily available when required. Always keep a selection of layout, cartridge and watercolour paper in the folder ready for use. Work should also be kept clean and flat. Always date any work and arrange according to different project themes. Have a folder of work ready to present at any time without having to scramble at the last minute for interviews or assessments.

Work should always be approached in a professional way. Often in design studios, students will have their own working area allocated to them with a drawing desk, and pin board on which to display research material.

MASKING FILM

Masking film is a transparent film used to protect areas on a drawing where colour is not needed. The film is low tack which means it can be removed without damaging the surface of the paper. When applying the film, the entire drawing should be covered and the areas to be coloured cut out with a scalpel. Great care should be taken when using a scalpel as it is extremely sharp.

SCHWAN STABILO

Drawings produced with a Schwan Stabilo black pencil using different pressures. Note the two stages illustrated:

1. Fineliner pen to outline the drawing.

2. Shading the line drawing with the pencil.

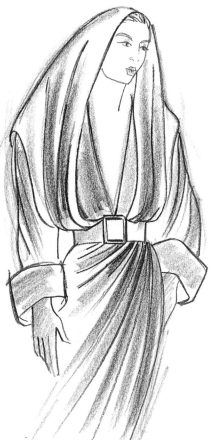

Here a smooth Bristol board was used for the finished illustration

1. A line drawing was produced working from a model

2. The shading was applied leaving areas of white to suggest the rich folds of the garment

1

2

3

4

Illustrations of knitwear and jeans produced with soft coloured pencils. A solvent spray has been applied using a cotton bud or paintbrush to soften the effect

COLOURED PENCILS

There is a wide range of coloured pencils, graded from soft to hard. They may be purchased in boxes with a large or small selection of colours, or obtained individually. Some are water-solvent and may be combined with water for application with a brush over the pencil, in order to give a watercolour effect.

Always experiment with these pencils before applying them to the drawing. The more pressure applied to the pencil, the deeper the tone and the more intense the colour will be. It is more effective to stroke in one direction only (as illustrated).

Select a paper, from rough to smooth depending on the effect required. Remember to use an absorbent paper when applying water.

Experiment with pencils

1. **Tone.** Use one colour to produce four colourways. Vary the squares from light to progressively darker tones.

2. **Burnishing.** Colour may be smoothed out by burnishing. This is achieved by going over the colour with a white or light grey pencil.

3. **Mixing colours.** Coloured pencils may be mixed to create a wide range of colours.

4. **Changing tones.** Tones of colours are made by changing the pressure on the pencils.

Coloured pencils used working in one direction, leaving areas of white to give contrast and depth

57

LINE DRAWINGS AND COOL GREY MARKER PENS

The sketches have been produced using a fine Artline Pen (0.4) in black. The tone has been applied using a cool grey Magic Marker felt-tipped pen (C.2). This technique is useful when you are required to develop sketches quickly.

Caran D'Ache neocolour

WAX AND WATER SOLVENT CRAYONS

A large and varied selection of wax crayons is available and they come in different thicknesses. They produce a solid bright colour and the harder the pressure, the deeper the tone, but it is difficult to produce different tones with wax crayons. Experiment with the crayons on paper of different textures and colours. Some crayons are wax based, others are water solvent and may be used combined with water.

A wax crayon or candle may be used as a resistant to watercolour. When a wax crayon or candle is used, the paper beneath the wax will be waterproof and the waxed area will remain free of colour.

Caran D'Ache Magic Marker for flesh tint – Barely Beige A822

Reeves wax crayons

Caran D'Ache neocolour wax oil

LINE DRAWINGS

The range of pens used for line drawing may be divided into five groups:

1. technical pens
2. plastic-tipped pens
3. fibre-tipped pens
4. roller pens
5. ball-point pens

New types are constantly being produced. When selecting a pen, experiment with it first to see if it produces the line required. The paper or card to be used also has to be considered carefully as the surface will affect the line value.

The drawings on these pages illustrate the use of different techniques using a variety of pens with different line values, often within the same drawing.

Drawing pens

Technical pens

The ink pens used by designers are known as technical pens. They produce a clear line, the nib of the pen being in the shape of a tube. The ink is fed down the tube, the size of which produces the width of the line. Technical pens are extremely accurate for very fine detailed work.

Plastic-tipped pens
These produce very fine accurate lines.

Fibre-tipped pens
The nibs are made from vinyl tip or nylon, and vary from firm to supple. They are made in a selection of sizes for different line values.

Roller pens
These have a very smooth action, producing an even flow ot ink. A range of colours and widths are available.

Ball-point pens
The point is made from a steel carbide ball that rolls, and is available in a range of colours and widths.

SCHWAN STABILO SOFT COLOUR

This is a smooth coloured pencil, giving intense rich even areas of colour without streaking. It can be used with turpentine, also combined with solvent based marker pens with highlight fastness and colour brilliance. Colour may be blended by applying layers on top of each other.

BLACK LEAD PENCILS

A large selection of black lead pencils are available in different thicknesses from hard to soft. The choice of paper and its texture is important depending on the effect required. A tough textured paper is needed for a tweed effect, and a smooth surface for a draped silk.

When working it is advantageous to have a selection of pencils, some sharpened to a fine point and others with a softer point for shading.

The pressure on the pencil gives a darker tone when shading, leaving areas of white to show the details. A white pencil may also be used.

WATERCOLOUR

Watercolour may be bought as a solid tablet or as a paste in a tube, and can be thinned with water. Paint boxes of different sizes are available and brushes of different quality and sizes are obtainable. Unless you are using good quality paper it should be stretched. If it is not stretched it will react to the water, cockle, and distort the work.

Stretching paper

Fill the sink with clean cold water. Pass the paper through the water, hold it up for a few seconds to let all the excess water run off, then lay it flat on the drawing board. Fix the paper down on the board with brown gumstrip round the edges. When the paper has dried it will be perfectly flat and ready for use. When the drawing is completed and perfectly dry, use a scalpel and straight edge rule to cut the paper from the board.

A completed design drawing ready for presentation. The working drawings from which it was developed are shown opposite.

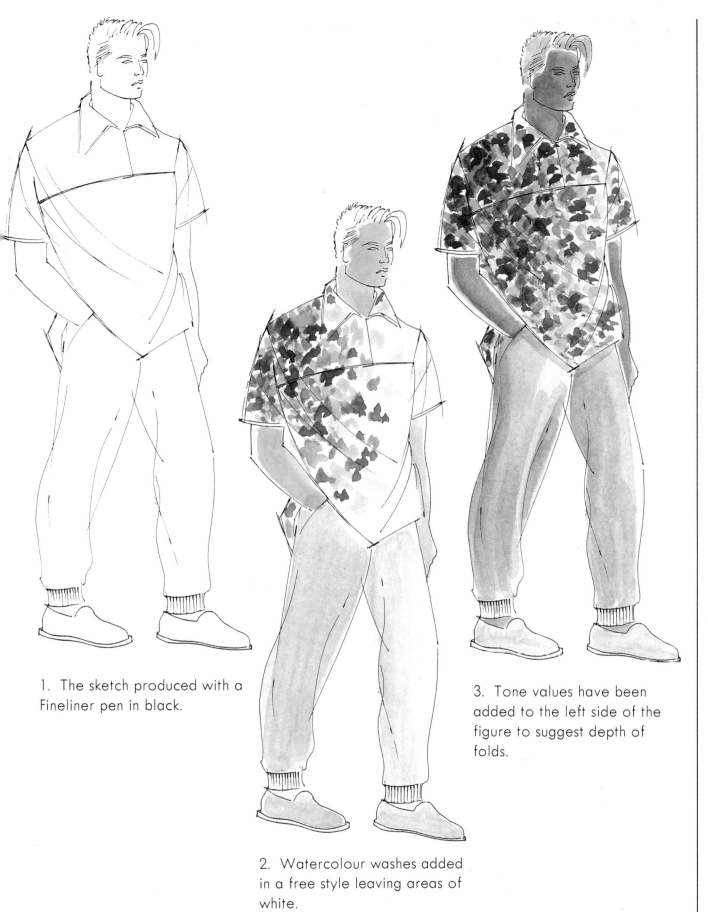

1. The sketch produced with a Fineliner pen in black.

3. Tone values have been added to the left side of the figure to suggest depth of folds.

2. Watercolour washes added in a free style leaving areas of white.

MARKERS

Choosing from the range of markers available can be bewildering. Some contain soluble ink and others permanent colour-fast ink. The nibs tend to be fibre-tipped nylon or foam. Sizes range from fine to broad, and they may be round, square, bullet or chisel shaped. They are also available in a wide range of colours. Note that the caps must always be replaced after use otherwise the pens tend to dry out. Spirit-based pens should always be used in ventilated areas.

Studio markers are also available in a wide range of colours and tones. Some are made with two nibs, broad and fine, combined on the one pen, and produce a clean smooth flat effect. They tend to be expensive, but looked after they will last a long time. Bleed-proof paper which prevents ink passing through on to the backing sheets, is available for use with permanent markers.

○ Markers tend to bleed on some papers and may go beyond a line. Always experiment with pens first before applying colour to an original drawing.
○ Some areas of the work will tend to look darker if these are gone over twice with the same marker.
○ Always clean the nib if one colour is to be used over another.

Using grey Pantone markers

Pale grey marker pens, when used on a line drawing to indicate a white fabric, are very effective. They may also be used to indicate the depth of a fold in the fabric, such as the shadow under the brim of a hat or gathers from a skirt or sleeve.

Note the way the grey pen is used to suggest the flowing folds of the skirt in this drawing. The effects of beading on the bodice and skirt are achieved by applying white paint.

71

Using coloured Pantone markers

Coloured Pantone markers can be applied to a template to build up depth of colour. Shading and texture are achieved by drawing in different directions and leaving areas of white.

THE USE OF MECHANICAL TINTS

A large selection of tints, of which Letratone are the most readily available, provide instant tones, textures and patterns. They may be purchased by the sheet and transferred onto the artwork by placing the tint over the area to be covered. The shape required is cut with a

sharp knife and the tint peeled off the backing paper. It is then placed on the drawing, first making sure that the surface is clean.

Lines may be drawn on the surface of the tint with a pen. White paint may also be applied to block out the tint to give certain effects.

By cutting with a sharp blade or knife it is possible to peel sections away to reveal the paper beneath.

These drawings show how percentage dot tints can be used to indicate skin tone and shading.

GOUACHE

Gouache is basically the same as watercolour but is mixed with white pigment, which makes it opaque.

Gouache used with water for blouse and flesh tints. The shorts are solid grey mix

Gouache, when dry, forms a positive film of colour, and sharp, hard divisions of solid colour are associated with it. A free style of painting may also be achieved where the brush strokes are visible. This illustrates working wet-on-wet, i.e. with wet paint on wet paper. Whatever method is used, the main characteristic is the ability to provide a strong contrast of colour and tone.

Watercolour boards or papers are most suitable for gouache. Tinted papers may also be used as the paint is opaque.

Solid colour

Dry brush

Mixed with water

PATTERN AND TEXTURES IN LETRATONE TINTS

A large selection of Letratone patterns are available. Illustrated are a few examples of patterns applied to line drawings. Note the different effects that may be achieved.

Fashion details of draped materials. Black lines are sketched in to indicate folds

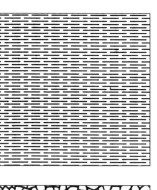

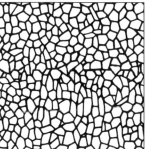

Pattern applied using areas of white for folds and gathers

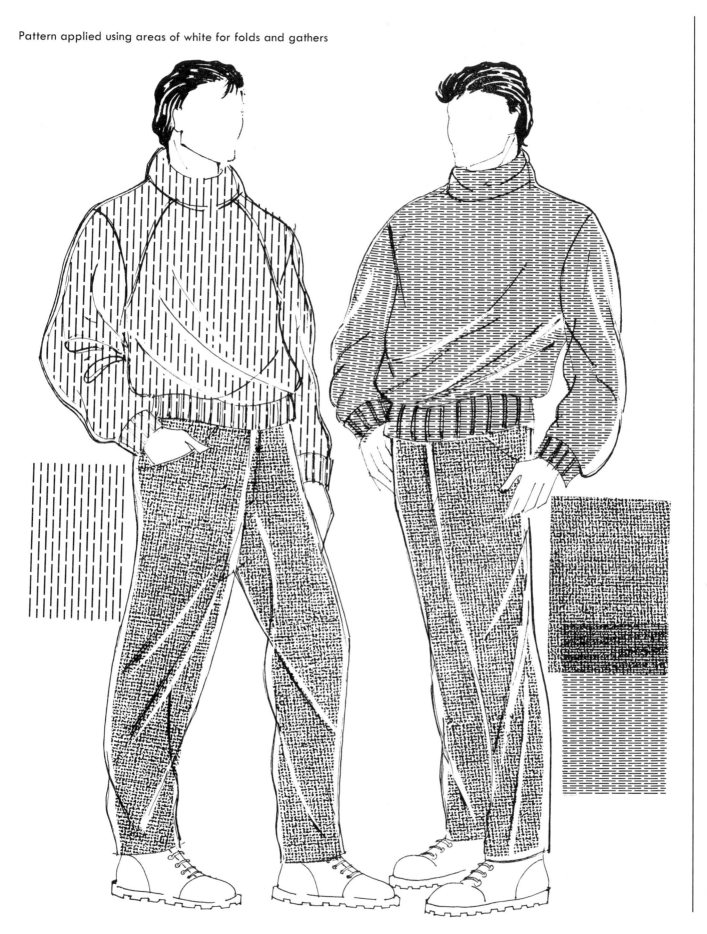

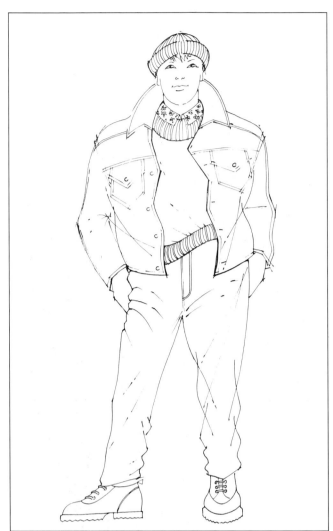

COLOURED PENCILS AND BLACK FINELINER PEN

The sketch has been produced in four stages.

1. The drawing was sketched with a black Fineliner pen on a smooth white illustration card.

2. The denim jacket and trousers were coloured with an ultramarine pencil, shaded in one direction from one side of the figure in a darker tone by putting more pressure on the pencil. This gives the effect of more light falling on one side of the figure.

3. In the final stage the darker tones were added to the garment under the collar, pocket, and folds in the jacket and trousers. A soft lead pencil has been used over the blue denim to give the effect of the texture and weave. The face was tinted with a burnt sienna pencil, shading the face on one side. A thick line has been added round the figure with a medium Stabilo black pen and burnished with a white pencil to smooth out the colour.

4. The drawing was completed with a thick black outline round the figure, the latter being cut out and mounted using a spray mount onto a clean sheet of card.

ACHIEVING TEXTURE IN PEN AND INK

Various textures may be achieved by using different line values in the same drawing. Examples are shown of herringbone, tweed, checks, ribbed and cable-stitch knitwear.

USING BACKGROUNDS

Black and white illustration showing the use of a background to complement the figure. Note the way in which the figure has been cut out leaving an area of white, giving added emphasis.

WATERCOLOURS AND FINE ARTLINER BLACK PEN

The sketches have been produced in four stages.

1. Sketched with a pencil on watercolour paper.
2. Colour washes applied using watercolour paints.
3. Darker tone values added for folds, gathers and details
4. In the final stage the details have been emphasized using a fine Artliner black pen.

Note the way in which the figure poses were developed — using the centre front line and balance line as a guide.

Window Mounting   Window cut-out of card with work mounted from the back

Flat Mounting   Work placed on card fixed with a good adhesive spray or gum

When displaying work for assignments, exhibitions and interviews, extra consideration should be given to the presentation. It is important that work is well mounted and arranged, to make it easy for the examiner to view.

The work may be mounted in two ways: flat or window. Flat mounting is effective for design sheets and presentation drawings. Window mounting is more suitable for embroidery, knitting or fabric samples. The work should be mounted on card or coloured paper which is complementary to the work.

MOUNTING WORK

The way in which work is presented will make an impression on the viewer.

When mounting, whether window or flat, the layout, colour and lettering, must be given careful consideration in order to achieve the desired effect.

Mounting card

A large selection of mounting card of different thicknesses, colours and textures is available. Consideration should be given to the weight of the card especially if the work is to be carried in a portfolio, as below.

Adhesive

Spray mount allows the work to be repositioned. Only one surface of the paper needs to be sprayed. Always make sure that the room in which the spraying is carried out is well ventilated. Direct the nozzle some 46 cm (18 in.) away from the paper and carefully spray the required surface. Apply work to be mounted onto card and lightly position, then smooth out by pressing a clean sheet of paper over the work.

COMPETITIONS

Students of fashion design often enter fashion competitions organized by industry, i.e. manufacturers, magazines and fashion houses. This gives students the opportunity to have designs accepted professionally. Financial awards are sometimes offered and opportunities given to travel and gain work experience. Publicity may follow the winning of a competition and this may be taken up by the national press, magazines or trade journals. Receptions are sometimes arranged for students to receive the prizes and meet the sponsors.

The competitions vary. Some sponsors ask for a design presentation only, others require the design presentation together with the made up garment. For the final presentation, the design is often presented on the catwalk at a fashion show.

The requirements are very specific, usually presented as a design brief stating exactly what is expected. This should include the size of the presentation sheet or board, type of sketches required, and budget costing if the design is to be made up.

87

PRESENTATION DESIGN BOARDS

1. Line drawing of children's holiday casual wear for a presentation board, produced with a Pentel pen. A thicker line value was added to emphasize different areas of the drawing.

2. The motifs of fish, birds and butterflies have been added to the sketches often reducing them to scale on a photocopy machine. Colour has been added by using Schwan Stabilo soft colour pencils. Note the free way in which they have been used leaving areas of white for emphasis.

3. The completed presentation board. The figures have been cut out and pasted down onto card with a background photograph to give depth and suggest a holiday environment.

4. The back views are added as simple line drawings.

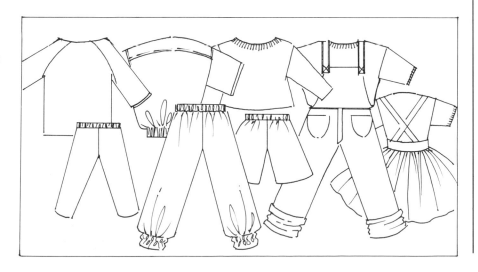

LAYOUT

The layout is a personal choice. When preparing work for presentation it is helpful to rough out variations of layout, considering carefully the information and work to be displayed before making the final decision. Often the layout is influenced by current fashion in graphics so it is useful to study the latest graphic and fashion magazines, marketing promotions and displays.

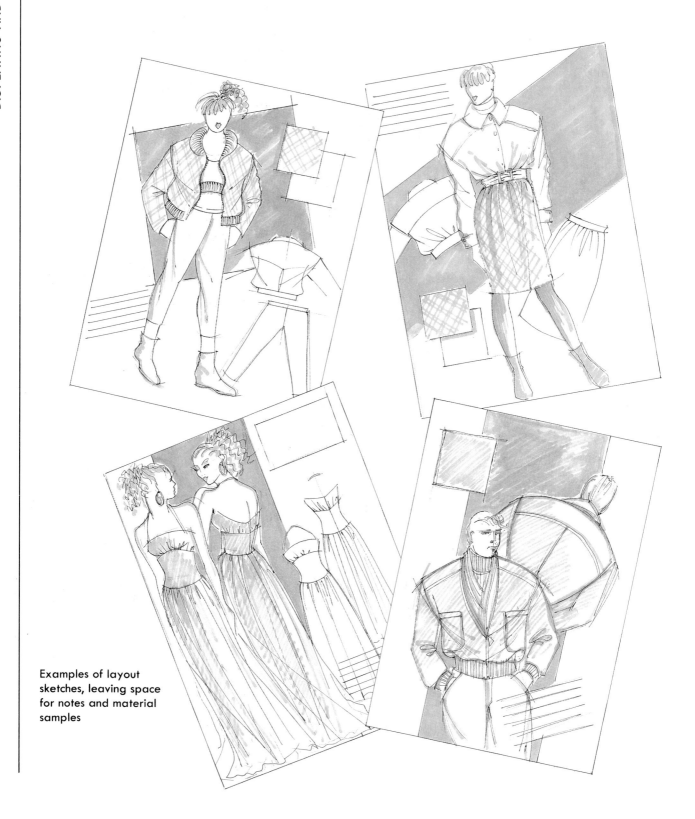

Examples of layout sketches, leaving space for notes and material samples

The final presentation

Marker pens and coloured pencils are used here to achieve the textured effects of the jacket and trousers, a thick black line is drawn round the figure which is cut out leaving a white line. This is effective when placed against the photograph.

PHOTOGRAPHIC BACKGROUNDS

This illustrates marker pens combined with coloured pencils. Note the way in which the cord trousers are suggested by the use of a black wax crayon. The jacket has a soft pencil line to suggest the texture of the fabric. The details are indicated with a Fineliner pen.

To complete the presentation, the figure has been cut out and pasted on to a coloured board. The photograph suggests the environment in which the garment could be worn.

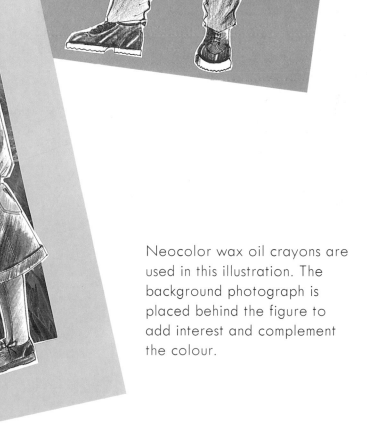

Neocolor wax oil crayons are used in this illustration. The background photograph is placed behind the figure to add interest and complement the colour.

FASHION ILLUSTRATION

Drake, Nicholas, *Fashion Illustration Today*, Thames & Hudson, 1987

Ireland, Patrick John, *Fashion Design*, Cambridge University Press, 1987

Ireland, Patrick John, *Fashion Design Drawing and Illustration*, Batsford, 1982

Ireland, Patrick John, *Encyclopedia of Fashion Details*, Batsford, 1987, 1989

Kumager, Kojiro, *Fashion Illustrations*, Graphic-Sha, 1988

Parker, William, *Fashion Drawing in Vogue*, Thames & Hudson, 1983

Yajima, Isao, *Figure Drawing for Fashion*, Graphic-Sha

Yajima, Isao, *Mode Drawing*, Atorie Ko

FIGURE DRAWING

Croney, John, *Drawing Figure Movement*, Batsford, 1983

Everett, Felicity, *Fashion Design*, Usborne, 1987

Gordon, Louise, *Anatomy and Figure Drawing*, Batsford, 1988

Loomis, Andrew, *Figure Drawing for all it's Worth*, Viking Press

Smith, Stan and Wheeler, Linda, *Drawing and Painting the Figure*, Phaidon, 1983

GRAPHICS

Dalley, Terence (Consultant Editor), *The Complete Guide to Illustration and Design Techniques and Materials*, Phaidon, 1980

Laing, J. and Davis R.S., *Graphic Tools and Techniques*, Blandford Press, 1986

Lewis, Brian, *An Introduction to Illustration*, The Apple Press, 1987

Welling, Richard, *Drawing with Markers*, Pitman, 1974

HISTORY OF FASHION

Blum, Stella, *Designs by Erté*, Dover Publications, New York, 1976

Boucher, Francis, *A History of Costume in the West*, Thames & Hudson, 1966

Davenport, Millia, *The Book of Costume*, Crown, New York, 1976

Ewing, Elizabeth, *History of Twentieth Century Fashion*, Batsford, 1992

Milbank, Caroline Reynolds, *Couture — The Great Fashion Designers*, Thames & Hudson, 1985

Murray, Maggie Pexton, *Changing Styles in Fashion*, Fairchild Publications, New York, 1989

O'Hara, Georgina, *The Encyclopaedia of Fashion*, Thames & Hudson, 1986

Peacock, John, *The Chronicle of Western Costume*, Thames & Hudson, 1991

Tilke, Max, *Costume Patterns and Design*, Magna Books, 1990

Note: *italics* refer to illustrations